KAWASAKI
WORLD'S FASTEST BIKE

rosen publishing's
rosen central
NEW YORK

MARY-LANE KAMBERG

For Rowin Rohrback

Published in 2014 by The Rosen Publishing Group, Inc.
29 East 21st Street, New York, NY 10010

Copyright © 2014 by The Rosen Publishing Group, Inc.

First Edition

Library of Congress Cataloging-in-Publication Data

Kamberg, Mary-Lane, 1948–
Kawasaki: world's fastest bike/Mary-Lane Kamberg.—First edition.
    pages cm.—(Motorcycles: a guide to the world's best bikes)
Includes bibliographical references and index.
ISBN 978-1-4777-1860-5 (library binding)—ISBN 978-1-4777-1874-2 (pbk.)—
ISBN 978-1-4777-1875-9 (6-pack)
1. Kawasaki motorcycle—Juvenile literature. I. Title.
TL448.K38K346 2014
629.227'5—dc23

                                                                              2013026250

Manufactured in the United States of America

CPSIA Compliance Information: Batch #W14YA: For further information, contact Rosen Publishing, New York, New York, at 1-800-237-9932.

CONTENTS

INTRODUCTION

Today, the Kawasaki Motors Corporation manufactures jet skis and all-terrain vehicles (ATVs). It's best known, however, for its motorcycles. The bikes have high horsepower, quick takeoff, and speed. In fact, Kawasaki builds some of the fastest bikes in the world.

Kawasaki Motors Corporation Japan started in 1924 as Kawasaki Aircraft. After World War II, the company created a new division for making engines for motorcycles. It built its first bike in 1954. Six years later, Kawasaki bought Meguro, the oldest motorcycle company in Japan and one of the top ten producers in the world. Kawasaki learned from Meguro's skills. In 1966, Kawasaki started an American corporation now known as Kawasaki Motors USA, based in Irvine, California.

Kawasaki has a reputation for high-performance bikes, including its best-selling Ninja sport bikes. It is also known for off-road, dual-sport, touring, and naked bikes.

Sport bikes are built for performance with racing technology. They have racy styling, are lightweight and fast, and steer and handle well. They stop fast. But comfort is not an issue.

Off-road bikes, called motocross bikes, are built to race in the dirt. These bikes have no headlights, taillights, mirrors, fairing, or windshield. They are illegal to ride on the street.

Naked bikes, also called standards, lack fairings and bodywork. They are bare-bones bikes that some riders think look mean and nasty, and they like them that way. A sport standard has a little more style. Riders sit a little more upright than on a pure naked bike.

Touring bikes include tourers and sport touring bikes. They are both built for road trips. The bikes are heavy, and they have soft seats. Speed is not a main focus, allowing riders to enjoy the trip, taking in scenery along the way. They appeal to older riders, so some riders call them "geezer gliders" or "old man's bikes." Sport tourers have the power and aerodynamics of a sport bike. They run faster than touring bikes, and they have a more comfortable ride than sport or naked bikes.

Overall, Kawasakis are built for fun—no matter how you define it.

The 1973 Kawasaki 900 Z-1 is the great-grandfather of today's Z1000. Nicknamed "The King," the bike has a four-cylinder, 903cc engine. It is the forerunner of all of today's superbikes, no matter the manufacturer.

CHAPTER ONE

THE WORLD'S FASTEST BIKE: NINJA ZX-14R

Do you have a need for speed? The Ninja ZX-14R is built for you. The 186-horsepower (hp), 1,441cc bike runs a quarter-mile (.40 kilometers) in 9.7 seconds and reaches 147 miles per hour (234 kilometers per hour) over that distance, according to *Cycle World*. At the drag strip, it speeds from 0 to 60 mph (96 kph) in 3.02 seconds, according to *Motorcycle USA*. That's why Kawasaki is known for the world's fastest motorcycle.

Some bikes go faster than the ZX-14R, but the Ninja gets fast faster. It's the "hardest-accelerating mass-production vehicle on our planet," said *Cycle World* in 2012. And *Motorcycle USA* called it "the most powerful production motorcycle we've ever tested."

The inline, four-cylinder ZX-14R is the flagship of Kawasaki's Ninja sport bike lineup. It was built for speed. But the four-stroke, liquid-cooled bike combines racetrack speed with comfort for the open road.

Reviewers describe the bike's acceleration as "mind-boggling" and "neck-snapping" with "oodles of oomph." In *Cycle World*, Nick Ienatsch reported that experienced riders on a test ride loved it. But inexperienced riders were "shocked and scared and shocked and scared, and that was just the first two gears. They got more panicked after that."

The Ninja ZX-14R was known as the world's fastest bike in 2013. Its "neck snapping acceleration" could shock, scare, and panic inexperienced riders. It was *Motorcycle USA*'s 2012 Motorcycle of the Year.

Motorcycle-USA.com named it the 2012 Motorcycle of the Year.

Power

The key to the fuel-injected ZX-14R's power boost is that the stroke is 0.16 inch (4 millimeters) longer than previous models. The stroke is the distance the piston moves inside the cylinder. Older models have only a 1,352cc capacity. The new

THE KING OF THE MIDDLE-WEIGHTS: 2013 NINJA ZX-6R

The Ninja ZX-6R first hit the streets in 1995. Kawasaki redesigned it in 2003 with a 636cc motor. The bike sold side by side with the 599cc Ninja ZX-6RR, which was built for racing. The ZX-6R outsold the racing version for three years. But the engine was too big for the racetrack. Kawasaki took it out of the lineup after 2006. It focused on racetrack riders.

In 2013, Kawasaki decided to bring back its ZX-6R. The factory wanted to appeal to more people. They wanted a bike for all riding levels. But it needed the get-up-and-go of the other Ninjas. Engineers wanted more engine capacity. One way to get that was to increase the inside of the engine's cylinder. However, the bike would be wider and heavier.

Instead, designers started with the 599cc ZX-6RR motor and added 0.1 inch (2.6 mm) to the stroke. The change added 37cc capacity without changing the engine size or weight. It gave the bike more power. The new design earned the "King of the Middleweights" title from Motorcyle.com.

65mm stroke added 89cc to the engine capacity at the same engine size and weight.

In a 2012 *Motorcycle USA* comparison, the Kawasaki "outpowered and outran" the comparable Suzuki Hayabusa and BMW. All that power, however, requires fuel. In the comparison, the Ninja got only 32.1 miles per gallon (51.7

kilometers per gallon). It had the worst gas mileage of the three bikes. However, the stock 5.8-gallon (22-liter) fuel tank means the bike could run about 186 miles (299 km) per tank, according to *Motorcycle USA*.

Handling and Comfort

The ZX-14R's frame is a hollow aluminum box. A frame is a bike's skeleton. It holds the engine, transmission, and suspension. On the Ninja, it arches from over the engine. It is narrow, strong, rigid, and light. The bike's ten-spoke wheels are also

Although it's built for speed, the ZX-14R handles well. The traction control system has three settings, so a rider can make adjustments according to road conditions and riding ability.

lightweight. However, the ZX-14R is a heavy bike. Its curb weight is 584 pounds (265 kg). Curb weight is the weight of a motor-cycle with standard equipment and fluids, but without a rider or cargo. It's also a long bike, with a 58.3-inch (148-cm) wheelbase.

A GENTLEMEN'S AGREEMENT

Speed sells. Speed also kills. How fast must riders go?

Before the 1980s, motorcycles with a 125-mph (201-kph) top speed satisfied most riders. In the mid-1980s, though, Kawasaki and Honda vied to make the world's fastest bike. In just three years, the top bikes went from 145 mph (233 kph) at the end of a half mile to 159 mph (256 kph).

By 1987, the U.S. Congress was paying attention. Senator John Danforth introduced the Motorcycle Safety Act. The bill died, and the quest for speed continued. By 1999, the Suzu-ki Hayabusa topped the world record at 194 mph (312 kph). Rumor had it that Kawasaki's next model year would bring a bike that could break the 200 mph (322 kph) mark.

In response, European officials started worrying about illegal racing. Talk of import bans against the superbikes spurred manufacturers to action. In 2000, manufacturers in Japan and Europe joined an unofficial—and unadmitted—"gentlemen's agreement." They put electronic limiters on their products to ensure top speeds of 186 mph (300 kph). Since then the world's fastest bike has been determined not by top speed, but by how fast it can get there.

Adam Waheed said in *Motorcycle USA*, "It feels like it was made specifically for taller than average riders. However with its low seat height of 31.5 inches [80 cm], smaller riders can handle it, too."

In fact, the bike handles surprisingly well. It's comfortable for long road trips. It takes sweeping turns with ease. The electronics package includes a traction control system with three settings—plus the choice to turn it off. Riders can change the setting based on skill or road conditions. The top two give the best traction in normal conditions. The second level also protects against unwanted wheelies and wheel spin. At the lowest setting the bike is easy to control, even on wet roads. The bike's adjustable suspension also improves traction. The multiple engine power modes offer riders more choices.

When Kawasaki introduced the ZX-14R in 2012, reviewers thought the powerful machine should have an antilock braking system. The next year, the manufacturer upgraded the stopping power with the ZX-14R ABS model.

All in the Family

Not everyone is ready for a 1,441cc rocket. Fortunately, the ZX-14R's Ninja siblings are fun and fast, too.

- The Ninja 300 has the lowest technology and the lowest-cost parts—and the lowest price. But it's the most fun. It's

The Ninja 300 has the lowest technology and the lowest price of the various Ninja sizes. It's a good bike for new riders, and it delivers the speed that experienced riders want.

easy enough to handle for less experienced riders. But it also delivers the speed that skilled racers enjoy.

- The Ninja ZX-6R's 636cc engine has a smaller version of its big brother's inline, four-cylinder power plant. The extra zip added in 2013 makes the bike easier to accelerate out of corners.
- The Ninja ZX-10R is no bike for beginners. The 998cc magnifies mistakes. "But," said *Motorcycle USA*, "all those other riders won't see them as you blow by in a flash of green."

CHAPTER TWO

DOWN AND DIRTY: KX450F

The three most important words for a motocross bike are performance, performance, and performance. The KX450F delivers all three.

In fact, a rider can buy it and race it right off the showroom floor. And the KX450F was born to race. Reviewers loved it:

- *Cycle World* called it a "true race bike," and said, "The more aggressively it's ridden, the better it works."
- RacerxOnline.com said, "Don't blame the bike if you can't win on a KX450F!"
- *Motorcycle USA* called it "the green meanie" and said "it just rips up the hills." It named it the Best Motocross Motorcycle in both 2011 and 2012.
- *Dirt Rider* called it "the best stock bike in its class." It won the magazine's 450 "shootout" comparison in both 2012 and 2013.

Motocross is a motorcycle race on a dirt track with hazards like muddy ruts, bumpy jumps, and rough, high-speed sections. Supercross is the same kind of race held in a stadium. Motorcycles that compete in these races are called dirt bikes. They are illegal to ride on the street. They lack lights, mirrors, and other features required on public roads.

Dirt bikes used for motocross racing have no lights, tachometer, or speed-ometer. They are illegal to ride on public streets. *Motorcycle USA* named the KX450F the Best Motocross Motorcycle in both 2011 and 2012.

Like other dirt bikes, the KX450F has no tachometer. So no redline appears on specification lists. However, some redline measurements have been reported. The 2011's redline, for instance, was reported on Motorcycle.com. Test rider Greg Jones said, "The redline is 12,500 rpm, and the rev limiter lets you know when you've exceeded it."

Without a tach, the rider must rely on the feel of the bike. When the rider reaches the maximum revolutions per minute (rpm), the rev limiter shuts down the acceleration. The increase in speed—but not the forward motion—abruptly stops.

Off to the Races

Motocross bikes have no speedometers, so speed is not officially measured. However, one race venue reported the 2012 KX450F's speed. Officials at the 2012 Tecate SCORE Baja 500 desert race clocked the bike at 49 mph (78.8 kph). It was the fastest bike on the course. The THR Motorsports Monster Energy Team led by Robby Bell won the race by two minutes and twenty-eight seconds. It was the first time in fifteen years that any bike beat a Honda in that race. Honda rolled in sixth, fifty-three minutes behind the Kawasaki team.

However, the Kawasaki team had some trouble. They might not have finished the race at all because the fuel tank was too small, and the team almost ran out of gas around Mile 58. "I kept stopping by locals at the side of the track, trying to get some gas," Bell said in *Cycle World*. "Finally, I found two that had some and who were more than happy to give me enough to get to pit two … It wouldn't have been much longer until I ran out."

Pros and Cons

Aside from the too-small fuel tank, another complaint is noise. *Dirt Rider* called the muffler "tragic" and added that it "sounds blown-out and raspy even when brand new." Writers at *Cycle World* complained a bit louder: "Loud pipes don't save lives; they close riding areas."

RYAN VILLOPOTO

It's hard to talk about motocross without mentioning Ryan Villopoto. He is one of the best motocross and supercross riders in history. The champion has never raced anything but a Kawasaki. As an amateur, he rode 85cc, 105cc, and 125cc Kawasakis. As a professional, he moved up to the Monster Pro Circuit Kawasaki KX250F in 2006. That year, he won both the 250 Motocross and the Motocross of Nations. He was named the Supercross/Motocross Rookie of the Year.

In 2009, his first year in the AMA Supercross Series, he rode a Team Kawasaki KX450F full-time. Villopoto broke his leg in a race in 2010, but returned to racing the next year. In 2011, he won six supercross races and placed in almost all the others to win his first supercross title. In 2012, he rode for the Monster Energy Kawasaki team. He took the super-cross championship. But he hurt his knee late in the motocross season and had to sit out the rest of 2012, as well as the 2013 AMA Motorcross Series.

Some of his outstanding accomplishments:

2009 - 2nd U.S. Open of Supercross
2009 - 6th Supercross
2010 - 4th AMA Supercross
2011 - 1st Monster Energy Cup
• 2011 - 1st Motocross of Nations
• 2011 - 1st AMA Motocross
• 2011 - 1st AMA Supercross
• 2012 AMA Supercross Champion
• 2012 World Supercross Champion
• 2012 - 1st AMA Supercross

As an amateur and professional motocrosser, Ryan Villopoto has raced Kawasaki dirt bikes from 85cc to 450cc. He was the Supercross/Motocross Rookie of the Year in 2006 and won six supercross titles in 2011.

Before the 2013 model, racers also complained about handling corners. But improved bracing in 2013 added stiffness. Riders reported the bike felt more stable than in past model years.

Another welcome feature helps racers get a great start off the line. The KX450F is the only production motocrosser with a Launch Control Mode (LCM) feature. The LCM improves traction for quick, consistent starts right out of the gate. Motorcycle.com called it "one of the best stock ignition systems in the motocross world."

Finally, the bike is a quick-change artist. It's easy to adjust the passenger "compartment." Riders of every ability can adjust the bike to their liking, no matter their height and weight. They can easily select a comfortable riding stance. Kawasaki gave the handlebars adjustable clamps for four positions. The foot pegs have two. The KX450F is the only bike in its class with moveable pegs as a standard feature, meaning they come with the bike. New owners don't have to pay extra for them.

The front suspension and digital fuel injection system are also adjustable. With a 248-lb (112-kg) curb weight and a wheelbase of 58.3 in (1.5 m), the KX450F needs firm suspension. Kayaba specifically designed the forks for Kawasaki. It uses pressurized air instead of metal coil springs. The pressure is easy to change right at trackside. The firm suspension also helps the bike handle better, especially at corners. These features keep the bike stable. That's important throughout a race day as the course gets rougher.

The digital fuel injection system has three settings that take only seconds to change. In addition to the standard, there is one for hard terrain and another for soft terrain. Again, a racer can make the adjustment right at the track as conditions change.

The liquid-cooled, four-stroke, single-cylinder 449cc engine provides easy-to-control power. This results in more push out of the corners that continues to the end of the straightaways. The disc brakes stand up to the power, thanks to im-

Kayaba designed air forks that use pressurized air instead of metal coil springs to give the KX450F firm suspension for better handling. Riders can adjust the suspension right at the race site.

provement on the 2013 model. Kawasaki installed new front brake pads for stronger braking. The rear brake has a lightweight, petal-type rotor.

Most of the revamped technology resulted from feedback from the factory race team. So, all in all, the KX450F delivers the power, handling, and speed that dirt racers want. The bike has proven itself on some of the most demanding motocross and supercross tracks in the world.

CHAPTER THREE

RUNNING OFF THE ROAD: DUAL-SPORT KLR650

It's a bit of an ugly duckling with a split personality. At best, kind reviewers call the design "simple" and "utilitarian." But they praise the KLR650's versatility both on highways and backwoods trails. Motorcycle-USA.com named it the "Best Dual Sport" in 2012.

It's a bike you can ride to the end of the pavement—and keep going. According to Motorcycle-USA.com, "If there's a road on a map, this bike can ride it."

Total Motorcycle agreed. "Wherever the destination, whatever the distance, over any kind of terrain … the KLR650 is the motorcycle to get you there in style and comfort," it said. "It continues its reputation for being more rugged, more reliable, and higher performing, delivering the ultimate in all-round fun."

The bike is an industry leader. In 2013, the manufacturer said it was the "best selling dual sport" seven years in a row. Kawasaki introduced the KLR650 in 1987 and left it almost unchanged for twenty years. In 2008, the factory redesigned it. Improvements included new fairing, instrument panel, suspension, turn signals, and a bigger radiator.

Still, the bike has little to write home about, according to critics. The 651cc single-cylinder, four-stroke engine is no high-performance motor. It puts out a less-than-impressive 31.6 hp at 3,500 rpm. The fork and shock are basic. There

Between 2006 and 2013, the Kawasaki KLR650 was the best-selling dual-sport bike on the market. In 2008, the factory redesigned the fairing, instrument panel, suspension, and turn signals and added a bigger radiator.

are front and rear disc brakes with excellent stopping power. But antilock brakes are not an option.

"It's a bike of compromises," said Motorcycle-USA.com, "doing nothing particularly great, but it does almost everything well."

Best Features

What the KLR650 has is resilience. It has proved itself on dirt and gravel fun rides, off-road events, and long-distance tours. It's also a good ride for going to and from work in city traffic.

The five-speed transmission is all riders need on any surface. The bike is no racer, but it goes plenty fast. Riders have reported speeds of 100 mph (161 kph) to 115 mph (185 kph). The bike handles well at both high and low speeds.

"The KLR650 feels comfortable around town," said TopSpeed.com, "but also on the savage, muddy terrains."

An engine guard keeps loose rocks and gravel from hurting the bike. And the bike can go onto any area open to licensed vehicles, thanks to its U.S. Forest Service–approved spark arrestor. The radiator keeps engine temperatures consistent. That sustains power during hard use. It also increases engine life.

The KLR650 is a big, heavy bike with a curb weight of 432 pounds (196 kg). Its wheelbase is 58.3 inches (148 cm). It has a semi-double cradle frame of high-tensile steel. That makes it heavy, but its rear subframe detaches for easy maintenance. Once it is removed, the rider has easy access to the rear shock, air box, and carburetor.

The technology is so easy to understand, most riders can work on their own bikes. Riders serving as their own mechanics can get help from a strong online community, sometimes called the "KLR cult." Rod Morris at Top Gun Motorcycles said the bike is "easy to work on and can be fixed with baling wire and J-B Weld." J-B Weld is a bonding agent similar to glue.

A 36-watt alternator powers the bright headlight. There's enough charge left over for any electronic gadgets that a rider wants to add.

The KLR650 climbs hills with ease and handles well in city traffic. Its simple design lets riders act as their own mechanics with help from an online community known as the "KLR cult."

Easy Rider

Despite the weight and so-so engine, the bike is easy to ride—especially off-road. The power is steady enough to climb hills and move around or over obstacles. Motorcycle-USA.com said it handles as if it were half its actual weight. Strong wheels with 0.16-inch (4-mm) spokes improve steering.

The seat shape and foam filling make for an easy ride, even on long road trips. The front fork contributes to the

TAKING THE SHOW ON THE ROAD

If you're planning a road trip on a KLR650, you'll want to carry stuff with you. Kawasaki offers a higher windscreen, a seat pad, and luggage to make the ride easy and more comfortable. The accessories include:

- Gel seat kit that covers the stock seat for extra comfort
- Tall windshield that is 4 inches (10 cm) higher than the standard screen
- Durable saddle bags and a soft top case with a water-resistant, rubberized vinyl finish
- Tank bag that mounts between the handlebars and rider
- Zippered nylon pouch that attaches to the handlebar crossbar
- Trans handlebar bag that holds 2 pounds (.91 kg) of soft goods; it mounts close to the instrument panel and leaves room for a tank bag as well

comfort. Its 0.16-inch (41-mm) telescopic front fork is stiff enough for both off-road and highway use. The tall fairing and hand protectors provide good wind protection at highway speeds. The 6.1-gallon (23-l) fuel tank can take the rider about 237 miles (381 km) between pit stops, according to Motorcycle-USA.com.

DUAL-SPORT RIDING EVENTS

Motorcycle clubs all over the United States offer dual-sport riding events to riders of all abilities. For instance, the Ironman Dual Sport Riding Club based in Chico, California, offers rides amidst the best scenery in Northern California and Nevada. Often, camping and lunch are included, or hotels are close. Here are some examples:

- **Crown Point Rally**
  Several routes are offered for this gathering of dual-sport riders in the foothills east of Chico, California. One is a technical course for hard-core dirt riders. Another stays in the dirt most of the time. A third runs along twisting pavement with great scenery.

- **Wildwood 400**
  Beginners to experts are welcome on this 400-mile (644-km) ride along a scenic course with one-half dirt and one-half pavement and graded dirt roads. The ride starts in Wildwood, California, and includes an overnight stay in Fortuna, California.

- **The Red Mountain 350**
  This two-day ride for experienced riders starts in Berry Creek, California. It features about 90 percent dirt trails through the Lassen and Plumas national forests. Terrain includes rock gardens and stream crossings. Riders spend the night in Chester, California, on Lake Almanor and return to Berry Creek the next day.

The biggest complaint that dual-sport riders have is the rear suspension. It has the same spring as the 1987 model. Some riders think it needs an upgrade. However, riders can buy replacement springs in at least three sizes.

Another issue is seat height. The KLR650's is 35 inches (89 cm). It's not the highest in its class, but Ron Lieback of *Ultimate Motorcycling* said, "The tall saddle had me on my toes with my 32-inch (81-cm) inseam, though I was able to get one foot flat at stops, so I was not uncomfortable."

The KLR650 is an economical bike for all uses. It can do it all. And as Motorcycle-USA.com said, "For dual-sport riders who simply want to trek anywhere the map shows a squiggly line and the promise of a path … the KLR650 will get you there."

CHAPTER FOUR

ON THE ROAD AGAIN: CONCOURS 14 ABS

The newly designed Concours 14 was hot. *Motorcyclist* magazine named it the Best Touring Bike of 2008 and again in 2009. *Cycle World* magazine called it the Best Sport Tourer of 2008 and again in 2009. They praised its versatility and fast acceleration. It was easy to handle and easy to park.

The fuel-injected 1,352cc motor was based on the ZX-14. The four-stroke, liquid-cooled, inline four sent the bike over the quarter-mile (0.40 km) in 10.52 seconds at 130.5 mph (210 kph), according to *Motorcyclist* magazine. So why did Kawasaki make so many changes for 2010? Because the bike was hot. Too hot.

Not hot like going viral. Hot like a blast furnace. Heat from the engine made riders hot all over, especially on the lower legs and upper body. The factory learned about the complaint in market research focus groups made up of their Concours 14 customers. They discussed their likes and dislikes.

Owners liked the Concours 14's performance. What they wanted was more rider comfort. After all, the bike was built for touring. That means hundreds of highway miles per ride. So, in 2010, Kawasaki Japan redesigned the Concours 14 with its customers in mind.

Customers talked, and Kawasaki listened. Concours 14 riders wanted more comfort and less engine heat. The factory revamped the touring bike in 2010. Improvements included a heat shield and better wind protection.

Built for Comfort

Designers first focused on keeping engine heat away from the rider. They sealed the open spaces in the fairing. They increased the radiator exhaust ducts and made the fairing wider. They also added a heat shield under the right foot peg. Finally, they added a guard to the exhaust pipe to keep the rider cool while the bike idled.

The new windshield was taller for better wind protection. It had four electronically adjustable positions. The screen returned to its lowest position when the bike turned off. On restart, the windshield returned to the rider's previous setting.

Tall windshields can cause air pressure to smack a rider's head, so designers added cuts to the bottom of the shield. The cuts sent airflow to vents near the instrument panel. The new design made the air pressure the same in front of and behind the windshield.

The new instrument panel was easy to read. A digital display between the speedometer and tachometer included a clock, fuel gauge, odometer, two trip meters, fuel level, mileage, gear position, and tire pressure.

Focus groups also asked for heated handgrips and higher mirrors. So Kawasaki made heated handgrips standard. The factory raised the mirrors 1.5 inches (40 mm). That made the rear view better, and the mirrors also helped block wind.

Give 'Em What They Want

Customers wanted to go more miles between stops for gas. They asked for a larger fuel tank. But a bigger tank meant more weight. The bike's curb weight was already 688 pounds (312 kg) on a 59.8-inch (1.5-m) wheelbase. Instead the factory added a fuel economy assistance mode. When the rider selects the option, the motor runs at maximum efficiency as long as the bike stays under 6,000 rpm and 30 percent throttle.

The system "just turned 36 mpg (58 kpg) into 42 mpg (67 kpg)," said *Motorcyclist* magazine. Many factors contribute to fuel efficiency, but Ron Lieback at UltimateMotorcycling.com claimed a 25 percent efficiency increase at speeds less than 80 mph (128 kph).

Additional user-friendly features included two water-resistant side cases. The lightweight cases are big enough to hold a full-face helmet. They sit close to the bike's center of gravity. So they

Customers liked the optional antilock braking system (ABS) available on the 2010 Concours 14. In 2011, Kawasaki made the brakes standard and changed the name of the bike to the Concours 14 ABS.

have little effect on how the bike handles. The cases are easy to take off when the rider reaches his or her destination. Attachment hooks at the front of the tank make it easy to add a tank bag, and there's a spot for an accessory case on the rear.

Focus groups liked the keyless ignition system. It used a device called a fob. The electronic fob let riders start the bike from 5 feet (1.5 m) away The problem was getting a spare fob

TOURING BIKER'S TERMS

According to TotalMotorcycle.com, here are some official and not-so-official definitions every touring bike owner should know:

bagger A motorcycle with saddlebags and other touring gear.

big slab Interstate highway; also called a super slab.

brick A very hard motorcycle seat.

cage A car, truck, or van.

dresser A motorcycle set up for long-distance touring.

power shower Riding in the rain without rain gear.

ride two up Carry a passenger.

true blue A biker who takes long road trips.

twisties Roads with many turns or curves.

that could be hidden on the bike for emergencies. A second fob stored on the motorcycle would be within that range. It would defeat the electronic security. A thief could jump on the bike, start it, and ride off. Kawasaki responded with a smaller spare fob with a range of only 4 inches (10 cm). A rider had to hold the spare that close to the ignition system to start the engine. The rider could hide the extra key on the bike without disabling the security.

The 2008 front suspension was another complaint, so Kawasaki added more oil to the fork tubes to keep the bike from bottoming out on bumps. Bottoming out means the suspension runs out of room and hits internal stops. The change also made steering easier, especially on twisting roads. To top it off, the six-speed transmission was easy to shift. Riders didn't have to shift at all once they got up to speed. They could enjoy the scenery without having to downshift all the time.

All the changes paid off. *Cycle World* magazine named the 2010 Concours 14 the Best Sport Touring Bike of the Year. For the next three model years, the Concours 14 included the 2010 improvements.

Moving Forward

In 2010, Kawasaki offered an optional antilock braking system. By 2011, it became standard. The bike's name was changed to the Concours 14 ABS. The ABS designation was also included on the 2012 and 2013 models.

The front and rear brakes link for more control. Stopping action depends on the pressure applied. The front and rear brakes always work in the correct ratio. Riders get a choice of two settings. The "standard mode" is best for sport riding. The "high combined mode" is best for touring and carrying a passenger. The brakes work together with Kawasaki's traction control system (KTRC). The KTRC senses changes in wheel spin and tells the engine to "back off" if the rear wheel loses its grip on the road. Together, the systems keep the bike stable. They also contribute to better safety on wet roads.

A reviewer known as Doctor Speedy reported his first ride on the 2013 Concours 14 ABS on YouTube. He described the brakes as "excellent." He also liked the bike's "awesome power." "It's not the lightest bike in the world," he said, "but it feels light once it's moving."

He liked the seat size and cushioning and the riding position. Instead of sitting upright, riders lean forward.

"It's not the fastest bike," he added, "but it's probably the most comfortable. You're going to want to go out and ride this bike!"

CHAPTER FIVE

RIDING THE Z1000

The Z1000 is a bare-bones street bike with the emphasis on "bare." *Motorcyclist* magazine called it a "superbike without the body work."

In the United States, the Plain Jane bike is called a naked bike or street fighter. In England, Australia, and other places with British influence, it's called a hooligan. In the motorcycle industry, it's called a standard. Naked bikes account for only a small market segment, but some motorcyclists love them.

Kawasaki introduced the Z1000's great-grandfather as the four-cylinder Z1 in 1973. It is the common ancestor of all of today's superbikes. Its nickname is "The King." Nothing mattered but speed, and it delivered. It was the first Japanese motorcycle to win an American Motorcyclist Association national title.

In 2003, the factory launched the first Z1000. It wanted to honor the old Z1. The focus was on speed with style. Some loved the bike, but others hated it. There was no middle ground. The bike had plenty of power. It went a quarter-mile (.40 km) in 10.73 seconds at 127 mph (204 kph) with a maximum speed of 150 mph (241 kph), according to *Super Street-Bike* magazine.

But it rode hard. Riders complained about its soft suspension and engine vibration. In 2007, the factory redesigned

The Z1000 is a standard motorcycle, also known as a naked bike, street fighter, or hooligan. Some riders think they look "mean and nasty" without a fairing or elaborate bodywork.

it. The goal was to make it more streetwise. The new model had better suspension and reduced vibration. The bike handled better. But *Super StreetBike* magazine called the update "more mild than wild." U.S. sales bottomed out. American dealers refused to import it in 2009.

Kawasaki went back to work with another redesign for 2010. This time the factory got it right. It came up with a lighter, more powerful bike. The 481-pound (218-kg) curb weight is 22 pounds (10 kg) lighter than the 2007 model. Some of the weight loss came from trading an aluminum backbone for the old steel chassis. And the patented quad exhaust pipes are each 1.5 pounds (.68 kg) lighter than earlier models, despite greater capacity.

More weight loss came from the newly designed 1,043cc inline, four-cylinder, four-stroke engine. It was specifically designed for the new frame. In fact, the motor is part of the frame. This design makes the frame smaller, simpler, and lighter. Designers added a fourth engine mount and put all mountings closer to the bike's center of gravity. These changes reduced vibration and improved the ride.

The new liquid-cooled, fuel-injected motor delivers 136 hp at 9,600 rpm. That's a 13 hp increase over the older model. Its top speed is 160 mph (257 kph),

Designers for the Z1000 made the engine part of the frame. That made the frame smaller and lighter. Placing the engine mounts close to the bike's center of gravity reduced vibration for a better ride.

according to VisorDown.com. The bike runs the quarter-mile (.40 km) in 10.6 seconds at 131 mph (210 kph), according to *Motorcyclist* magazine. "You almost feel like you're due for a nosebleed when riding it," a member of the magazine staff said. "That is, until you enter the powerband and get thrust into the next time zone." The powerband is the rpm range

ELECTRIC MOTORCYCLES: COMING SOON? THEY'RE HERE!

Electric motorcycles are back. Interest in them is growing among manufacturers. They are spending time and money on research and development.

The first electric motorcycles were introduced in 1911. They ran 75 to 100 miles (121 to 161 km) per charge. They started easily and ran silently. However, bikes with internal combustion engines won the day. The public lost interest.

Today, concern for the environment, as well as the price and supply of oil, has renewed the appeal of electric bikes. In 2009, two American start-up businesses, Zero Motorcycles and Brammo, introduced modern versions. The Zero S is a naked bike. Brammo produces two off-road models and two legal for the street. Brammo also manufactures a model specifically designed for security and law enforcement fleets.

If demand grows, watch for major motorcycle manufacturers like Kawasaki to follow soon.

where the engine has the most power.

One complaint about the new version, however, is the maximum power doesn't kick in until the engine exceeds 10,000 rpm. According to *Motorcyclist* magazine, the rider has to rev it: "(You have to) blur through the gears at every stoplight and freeway on-ramp–and while that's great for a track day or street-racing your buddy, it's a big demerit for everyday riding."

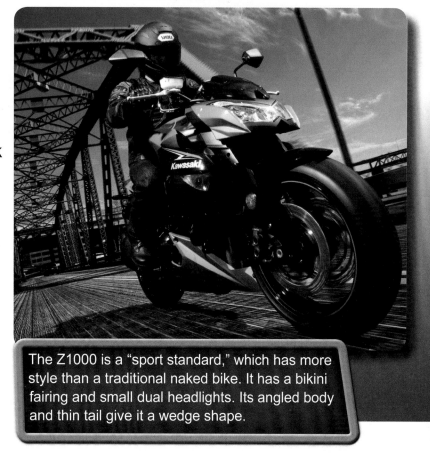

The Z1000 is a "sport standard," which has more style than a traditional naked bike. It has a bikini fairing and small dual headlights. Its angled body and thin tail give it a wedge shape.

Other complaints include the small, hard seat. It is comfortable enough for commuting to work but too hard for a long road trip. The forward riding position also reduces comfort on an all-day ride. The 32.1-inch (81.5-cm) seat height is more comfortable for tall riders than short ones.

The under-seat storage area is small. And there's little room for luggage—a tank bag and a small backpack at best. And although the handlebars are farther back and easy to reach, some riders think the handlebars could be a bit wider.

COMPARING THE 1973 KAWASAKI Z1 TO THE 2010 KAWASAKI Z1000

The Z1 is the granddaddy of today's superbikes. Here's how it compares with the new Z1000:

	Z1	Z1000
Price New	$1,895 in 1973	$10,499 in 2010
Curb Weight	542 lbs / 246 kgs	481 lbs / 218 kgs
Horsepower	67 bhp at 7,000 rpm	118 bhp at 8,750 rpm
Quarter-mile	13.1 sec. at 102 mph / 164 kph	10.5 sec at 132.5 mph / 213 kph
Brakes	Dual disc front, drum rear	Triple discs
Wheelbase	57.7 inches / 1.46 meters	58.5 inches / 1.48 meters
Engine capacity	903cc	1,043-cc
Engine type	Air cooled / carburetor-fed	Liquid cooled / fuel injected
Fuel capacity	4.7 gal / 18 l	4 gal / 15 l
Top speed	135 mph / 217 kph	160 mph / 257 kph

Sources: *Motorcyclist* magazine and MotorcycleClassics.com

The 1973 Kawasaki Z1 was the first Japanese motorcycle to win an American Motorcyclist Association national title. The factory revisited the model in 2003, 2007, and 2010.

On the positive side, improved handling makes the Z1000 fun to ride on winding roads. Plus, the bike looks good. Its styling has smaller dual headlights and a bikini fairing. It has a wedge shape, with an angled body and thin tail. The instrument cluster is an LCD panel with speedometer, odometer, trip meter, water temperature gauge, fuel gauge, and clock. The rider can adjust the panel three ways for the best view.

Improved brakes include four-piston front brakes and 9.84-inch (250-mm) rear disc brakes that are 1.2 inches (30 mm) larger than the previous model. The Z1000 was the first in its category to use radial calipers and radial front master cylinder.

Still, American dealers remained skeptical. "The new Z1000 almost didn't make it to the United States," said Justin Fivella in *Super Streetbike* magazine. "Due to its unsuccessful predecessor, the powers that be at Kawi of North America repeatedly denied Kawi Japan's requests to bring the bike over…until they rode it. One spin around the test track and the U.S. side of Team Green was sold."

So were *Cycle World* magazine's judges, who named the Z1000 the Best Standard in both 2010 and 2011. The bike also won the 2011 *Australian Motorcycle News* Shootout against the Yamaha FZ1 and the Triumph Speed Triple.

The bike offers good value for its price. "You'd be hard-pressed to find a better street bike than the new 2010 Kawasaki Z1000," said *Super Streetbike* magazine. "Simply put, you won't get this much performance for your buck anywhere else."

SPECIFICATION CHART

NINJA ZX-14R

Speed	186 mph / 300 kph
Redline	11,000 rpm
Horsepower	183.9 hp at 10,200 rpm
Torque	120 lb-ft at 7,500 rpm
Transmission	6-speed
Fuel capacity	5.8 gallons / 21.9 liters

KX450F

Speed	Not measured
Redline	Not measured
Horsepower	45.88 hp at 9,000 rpm
Torque	29.28 lb-ft at 7,200 rpm
Transmission	5-speed
Fuel capacity	1.64 gallons / 6.20 liters

KLR650

Speed	115 mph / 185 kph
Redline	8,000 rpm
Horsepower	31.6 at 6,100 rpm
Torque	30.13 lb-ft at 3,500 rpm
Transmission	5-speed
Fuel capacity	6.1 gallons / 23.1 liters

CONCOURS 14 ABS

Speed	186 mph / 300 kph
Redline	10,500 rpm
Horsepower	156 hp at 8,800 rpm
Torque	102 lb-ft at 6,200 rpm
Transmission	6-speed
Fuel capacity	5.8 gallons / 21.9 liters

Z1000

Speed	160 mph / 257 kph
Redline	11,500 rpm
Horsepower	136 hp at 9,600 rpm
Torque	81 lb-ft at 7,800 rpm
Transmission	6-speed
Fuel capacity	4 gallons / 15 liters

GLOSSARY

BOTTOM OUT What happens when the suspension runs out of room and hits internal stops.

CURB WEIGHT The weight of a fueled vehicle with standard equipment and fluids, but without a rider or cargo.

FLAGSHIP The best, largest, or most important item in a series or network.

FRAME A motorcycle's skeleton. The transmission, suspension, and sometimes the engine all attach to the frame.

GENTLEMEN'S AGREEMENT An informal oral or written agreement among two or more parties; it cannot be enforced but depends upon the "gentlemen's honor."

HOOLIGAN A standard or "naked" motorcycle.

J-B WELD A bonding agent similar to glue.

MOTOCROSS A motorcycle race held on a dirt track.

POWER The amount of torque an engine can create over time.

POWERBAND The rpm range where the engine has the most power.

REDLINE The highest revolutions per minute of the engine crankshaft that is considered safe.

REVS Revolutions. Measured as revolutions per minute (rpm), the higher the revs, the greater the speed.

STANDARD FEATURES Equipment that comes with the bike for the retail price; also called "stock" features.

TORQUE The force needed to make something turn.

TRACTION A tire's grip on the road

WHEELSPIN The rotation of a wheel without traction or with poor traction.

FOR MORE INFORMATION

American Motorcyclist Association (AMA)
13515 Yarmouth Drive
Pickerington, OH 43147
(614) 856-1900
Web site: http://www.americanmotorcyclist.com
The AMA is an organization that promotes the motorcycle lifestyle.
  It sanctions motorsport competitions and recreational events and
  represents motorcyclists' interests in the halls of government.

Canadian Motorcycle Association (CMA)
605 James St. North, 4th Floor
Hamilton, ON L8L 1J9
Canada
(905) 522-5705
Web site: http://www.canmocycle.ca
 The CMA is Canada's national association for motorcyclists. Its af-
  filiated clubs promote more than five hundred activities per year.

Federation Internationale de Motocyclisme (FIM)
International Motorcycling Federation
11 Route de Suisse
1295 Mies
Switzerland
+41 (0) 22 950 95 00
Web site: http://www.fim-live.com
The FIM is the international organization that governs motorcycle world championships in road racing, motocross, trial,
  endure, and track racing. It also engages in tourism, public
  affairs, and other activities linked with motorcycles.

L'Association Canadienne de Motos Anciennes
Canadian Vintage Motorcycle Group
33 Station Road
Toronto, ON M8V 2R1
Canada
Web site: http://www.cvmg.ca
The Canadian Vintage Motorcycle Group is a nonprofit organization
   of more than 2,200 members that promotes the use, restoration,
   and interest in older motorcycles and those of historic interest.

Motorcycle Industry Council (MIC)
2 Jenner Street, Suite 150
Irvine, CA 92618-3806
(949) 727-4211
Web site: http://mic.org
The Motorcycle Industry Council represents more than three
   hundred manufacturers and distributors of motorcycles,
   parts, and accessories. It is a nonprofit, national trade association for the U.S. motorcycle industry.

WEB SITES

Due to the changing nature of Internet links, Rosen Publishing has developed an online list of Web sites related to the
subject of this book. This site is updated regularly. Please use
this link to access the list:

http://www.rosenlinks.com/MOTO/Kawa

FOR FURTHER READING

Cain, Patrick G. *Moto X Best Trick*. Minneapolis, MN: Lerner Publishing Group, 2013.

Cain, Patrick G. *Moto X Freestyle* (Extreme Summer Sports Zone). Minneapolis, MN: Lerner Publishing Group, 2013.

Chaplain, John, and John Somerville. *Speedway Superheroes*. Somerset, England: Halsgrove, 2012.

Crosby, Graeme. *Croz Larrikin Biker*. Auckland, New Zealand: HarperCollins, 2011.

DeWitt, Norm, and Alan Cathcart. *Grand Prix Motorcycle Racers: The American Heroes*. Minneapolis, MN: Motorbooks, 2010.

Dixon, Franklin W. *The Hardy Boys Motocross Madness*. New York, NY: Aladdin Books, 2012.

Holter, James. *Dirt Bike Racers*. Berkeley Heights, NJ: Enslow Publishers, 2010.

Kresnak, Bill. *Motorcycling for Dummies*. Hoboken, NJ: Wiley Publishing, 2008.

LaPlante, Gary. *How to Ride Off-Road Motorcycles: Key Skills and Advanced Training for All Off-Road, Motocross, and Dual-Sport Riders*. Johannesburg, South Africa: Motorbooks, 2012.

McDiarmid, Mac. *Mick Grant: Takin' the Mick*. Somerset, England: Haynes Publishing, 2012.

Oxley, Mat. *The Fast Stuff: Twenty Years of Top Bike Racing Tales from the World's Maddest Motorsport*. Somerset, England: Haynes Publishing, 2012.

Stein, John L. *The Complete Idiot's Guide to Motorcycles*. New York, NY: Alpha Books, 2011.

Tieck, Sarah. *Superbikes*. Minneapolis, MN: Big Buddy Books, 2011.

Von Finn, Denny. *Drag Racing Motorcycles* (Torque: World's Fastest). Danbury, CT: Children's Press, 2011.

BIBLIOGRAPHY

Blackbourn, Rob. "Naked Pleasure." *Australian Motorcycle News,* Vol. 61, No. 13, January 4, 2012, pp. 1–4.

Burns, John. "Fifty Years of 'Do You Have Any Idea How Fast You Were Going?'" *Cycle World*, Vol. 51, No. 3, March 2012, pp. 40–45.

Fivella, Justin. "Used and Reviewed: 2003–2008 Kawasaki Z1000." *Super StreetBike*, December 2009. Retrieved January 30, 2013 (http://catalog.jocolibrary.org/cgi-bin/ezproxy /ezproxylogin?url=http://web.ebscohost.com/ehost/pdfviewer /pdfviewer?vid=7&sid=33f5cdd2-fb20-4037-a3ec-dc8453 a8997d%40sessionmagr10&hid=25).

Henshaw, Peter. *How Your Motorcycle Works*. Dorchester, England: Veloce Publishing, 2012.

Hutchinson, Ken. "2012 Kawasaki ZX-14R First Ride." *Motorcycle USA*, December 26, 2011, Retrieved February 28, 2013 (http://www.motorcycle-usa.com/157/11838/Motorcycle -Article/2012-Kawasaki-ZX-14R-First-Ride.aspx).

Ienatsch, Nick. "Kawasaki ZX-14R: Everything Else Is Officially Slow." *Cycle World*, Vol. 512, No. 3, March 2012, pp. 34–38.

Kunitsugu, Kent. "Give 'Em What They Want." *Sport Rider*, March 2010, pp. 50–54.

Lieback, Ron. "2012 Kawasaki KLR650 Commuter Test." *Ultimate Motorcycling*, May 6, 2012. Retrieved March 16, 2013 (http://ultimatemotorcycling.com/2012-kawasaki-klr650 -commuter-test).

Lieback, Ron. "2013 Kawasaki Ninja ZX-14R ABS Preview." *Ultimate Motorcycling*, September 15, 2012. Retrieved February 28, 2013 (http://ultimatemotorcycling.com/2013 -kawasaki-ninja-zx-14r-abs-preview).

Motorcycle-USA.com. "Best Dual Sport 2012: Kawasaki KLR650." December 27, 2012. Retrieved January 30, 2013 (http://www.motorcycle-usa.com/586/15144/Motorcycle -Article/Best-Dual-Sport-2012-kawasaki-KLR650.aspx).

Szulewski, Tricia. "Gaining Traction." *RoadBike*, January/February 2010, pp. 22–26.

Waheed, Adam. "2012 Kawasaki Ninja ZX-14R Comparison." Motorcycle-USA.com, April 30, 2012. Retrieved January 28, 2013 (http://www.motorcycle-usa.com/156/12925/Motorcycle -Article/2012-Kawasaki-Ninja-ZX-14R-Comparison.aspx).

INDEX

About the Author

Mary-Lane Kamberg is a professional writer specializing in nonfiction for young readers and adults. She used to ride a 125cc Suzuki TS125 street-trail bike on- and off-road with her husband.

Photo Credits

Cover, p. 1 Nildo Scoop/Shutterstock.com; pp. 5, 38 Source Interlink Media/Getty Images; pp. 7, 9, 14, 18, 20, 22, 27, 29, 34, 35, 37 Photos courtesy of Kawasaki Motors Corp., U.S.A.; p. 12 Fast Bikes Magazine/Future/Getty Images; p. 16 Jeff Bottari/Getty Images; interior pages background elements Dudarev Mikhail/Shutterstock.com, Yuriy_fx/Shutterstock.com; back cover © iStockphoto.com/JordiDelgado.

Designer: Brian Garvey; Editor: Bethany Bryan; Photo Researcher: Marty Levick